**DIESTERWEGS
NEUSPRACHLICHE
BIBLIOTHEK**

William Golding

Lord of the Flies

Teacher's Book

by
Dieter Smolka

D1663164

VERLAG MORITZ DIESTERWEG
Frankfurt am Main

"…." (89,6) = Zitat aus dem Text, direkte Rede
(Seitenangabe, Zeilenangabe)

'….' (90,5) = Zitat aus dem Text, aber keine direkte Rede
z.B. bei Beschreibungen etc.

ISBN 3-425-09846-2

© 1992 Verlag Moritz Diesterweg GmbH & Co., Frankfurt am Main.

Satz: Satzherstellung Karlheinz Stahringer, Ebsdorfergrund
Druck- und Bindearbeiten: Weihert-Druck, Darmstadt

Contents

Introduction

Amnesty International regularly points out the horrors, inhumanity and cruelty that vast numbers of people have to endure in dictatorships and totalitarian states all over the world today. These people are oppressed, tortured, and killed by their fellow people.

William Golding's message is a call for human solidarity, humanity, social responsibility and critical self-awareness. The Teacher's Guide to the interpretation and analysis of *Lord of the Flies* presents the essentials of the novel and points out its significance for today's world.

I would like to thank my friends and colleagues who have contributed many valuable ideas. In particular, I would like to thank Bärbel Gross, John Poziemski and Kerry Barber for their critical assessment and contributions.

January 1992   Dieter Smolka

Chapter 1: The Sound of the Shell

Summary Headlines

1. The world is at war. A plane with evacuated children is attacked and crashes into a jungle on an island.
   Ralph and Piggy meet. (p. 5, l. 1–p. 13, l. 29)
2. Ralph and Piggy find a shell. Ralph blows the conch, and more boys appear on hearing the sound of the shell. (13,30–17,30)
3. Jack Merridew and the choir boys arrive. (17,31–20,19)
4. The first meeting is held. Ralph is voted chief. (20,20–21,36)
5. The first expedition is undertaken by Ralph, Jack and Simon. (22,1–30,5)

Significance

1. The main themes of *Lord of the Flies* are introduced in the very first chapter:
   – the conflict between good and evil,
   – the quest for power,
   – the potential cruelty lurking behind the innocent appearance of people.
   The following questions are raised:
   – Will the boys be able to establish a democratic and peaceful society?
   – Will they be able to find food, organize shelter and cope with rivalry, conflicting ideas, irrational fears, arrogance, ambition and the quest for leadership?
2. The lonely island appears to be a paradise. The setting parallels and contrasts the world outside with the children's world on the island. While the world is at war, the children try to establish a peaceful society on the island.
   It soon becomes obvious, however, that complex psychological, social, moral and political conflicts present in modern societies also form part of the children's world on the island; in the end their 'society' degenerates into violence and savagery.
3. The boys' expedition already reveals the potentially destructive force behind the innocent appearance of the children. This force eventually leads to the destruction of the island and of their society.

Guides for Analysis

1. How is the setting described?
2. How are Ralph and Piggy characterized?
3. Analyse the importance of the conch.
4. What does the arrival of the choir boys reveal?
5. Analyse the significance of the voting.
6. Analyse the significance of the first expedition.

1. How is the setting described? (5,1–27,33)

The world at war is contrasted with the 'coral island' (13,11). It is significant, however, that the island's pristine beauty has already been spoilt by the passenger tube — 'the long scar smashed into the jungle was a bath of heat'. (5,4–5) In Ralph's view the island is a dream come true, 'the imagined but never fully realized place leaping into real life.' (13,25–26) He is not concerned about possible dangers on the island and holds the naive belief that his father will soon come and rescue them.

Unlike Ralph, Piggy perceives the island as a dangerous place. He is worried and concludes rather pessimistically that "we may stay here till we die." (12,33)

These two contrasting perceptions reveal the ambiguity that exists on this apparent island paradise. There are traces of menace in the 'skull-like coconuts,' (8,24) the intense heat and in the comparison of the island to a boat 'moving steadily astern' (27,33) — indications of what lies ahead for the boys.

2. How are Ralph and Piggy characterized? (5,1–13,29)

The two boys are quite different in character, appearance, social background and attitude towards the new surroundings. Ralph is 'the fair boy,' (6,4) athletically built. He 'might make a boxer,' (8,30–31) but 'there was a mildness about his mouth and eyes that proclaimed no devil.' (9,1)

Ralph is delighted by the new experience on the island, which he enjoys 'with bright, excited eyes.' (9,6) He seems to be self-confident and optimistic but also naive and romantic. He comes from a privileged, probably upper middle-class family.

Piggy comes from a less privileged social background. He is the ugly and 'fat boy.' (6,7) He is a worrier, physically weak and self-conscious.

He has difficulty in moving through the undergrowth and cannot swim. He suffers from asthma, which makes him an object of ridicule to the others—Ralph: "Sucks to your ass-mar!" (11,30) He wears glasses and is forever cleaning them. Piggy wants to be accepted by Ralph and would like them to become good friends. Although Piggy appears to be frightened, he is a rational thinker and feeds ideas to Ralph. He keeps asking critical questions about their situation and what they should do. He makes logical and rational suggestions—"We ought to have a meeting." (9,21) However, he cannot stop Ralph's daydreaming.

Later in the novel, when the society of the boys begins to degenerate, Piggy's intellectual and rational influence on Ralph grows stronger. By the end of the novel, Ralph has gained a mature knowledge of himself and the world around him. He fully appreciates Piggy's friendship, which he never really accepted before. In the final part of the story Ralph comes to realize 'the end of innocence, the darkness of man's heart, and the fall through the air of the true, wise friend called Piggy.' (193,29–30)

3. Analyse the importance of the conch. (13,30–16,5)

Ralph's and Piggy's first reactions to the conch are quite different. Ralph takes a rather detached view of the matter: according to him the conch is an 'interesting and pretty and a worthy plaything.' (14,12–13) Not so Piggy: 'Piggy was a-bubble with decorous excitement,' (14,1) "It's ever so valuable." (14,4) He immediately discerns its practical value and suggests calling a meeting with it. This shows that Ralph is not as quick as Piggy to see the potential significance of the conch as a means of organizing civilization on the island.

The conch is used as a signal to the boys that they should congregate and as a means of obtaining free speech. It quickly develops into a symbol of democratic order and authority.

"It calls them away from primitiveness and toward awareness." (Meitcke 28)

It should be noted that in Greek mythology, Triton, Neptune's son, uses a conch to stir or calm the sea. The metaphorical link to *Lord of the Flies* is striking. By means of the conch, Ralph is able to control the boys' behaviour and to focus their attention during the assemblies.

However, the conch seems to be extremely fragile—Piggy: "Careful! You'll break it." (14,10) This reflects the fragility of the order that Ralph and Piggy are striving to establish.

4. What does the arrival of the choir boys reveal? (17,31–20,19)

The arrival of the choir boys differs from the individual and casual arrival of the other boys who have already gathered.

'Something dark' (17,31) appears. The 'creature' (18,1) is a group of boys dressed—'hidden' (18,7)—in black cloaks and wearing black caps. The description introduces an atmosphere of evil and menace and anticipates the 'incantation of hatred' (173,31–32) to come at a later stage in the novel.

The choir boys are organized along authoritarian lines. From Piggy's reaction—he 'asked no names' (19,13)—it is obvious that he feels intimidated by 'this uniformed superiority' (19,13) and the 'offhand authority' (19,14) of its leader, Jack Merridew.

"The marching choir, and the way Jack treats it, recalls an army world of authority, arrogance and callousness, rather than the holy singing their uniform suggests." (Kinkead-Weekes 24)

From his first appearance it is apparent that Jack is a strong-willed, self-confident person, 'who knew his own mind.' (20,1–2) He shouts orders at the choir boys, who 'huddle into line' (19,1) obediently. With his black cloak flying Jack vaults onto the platform, resembling a huge bat and conveying an aura of blackness and darkness.

Ralph's group, the democratic one, is characterized by its heterogeneity and individuality. Jack's group, the authoritarian one, is characterized by its uniformity, obedience and strict organization. In more general terms, these two groups may stand for different political systems, for democracy and dictatorship. Thus a conflict between these two groups is inevitable.

5. Analyse the significance of the voting. (20,20–21,36)

Most of the boys regard the 'toy of voting' (21,1) as pleasing. Jack and Ralph are seen as having outstanding leadership qualities and group appeal. Jack is the "chapter chorister and head boy. I can sing C sharp." (20,28) Ralph is marked out by 'stillness,' (21,5) 'size' (21,6) and 'attractive appearance.' (21,7)

Golding's implied comments on the essential ingredients of leadership are obviously meant ironically, alluding to the irrational way of decision-making in politics in any society. He illustrates how a crowd of uncritical and naive people—in this case: the boys—can easily be manipulated by irrational arguments as well as by the outward appearance and the assumed authority of a single person.

Ralph wins over the majority and is voted chief as he is in possession of the symbol of authority and power: the conch. Jack's reaction illustrates how he feels humiliated because he has lost out in his quest for power; his face 'disappeared under a blush of mortification,' (21,23) he 'started up, ... the air rang.' (21,24)

Realizing that Jack is a bad loser, Ralph is 'eager to offer something' (21,25) in order to establish an amicable relationship between himself and Jack. Thus, the choir is appointed the role of hunters. Having straightened out their role status, Jack and Ralph smile at each other 'with shy liking.' (21,35) This suggests that, while the two boys may have something in common, the rivalry between them will be a permanent issue in their relationship.

6. Analyse the significance of the first expedition. (22,1–30,5)

Ralph, Jack and Simon set out on an expedition to explore the island. They associate the expedition with
– delight and happiness:
  'A kind of glamour was spread over them ... and they were ... made happy by it.' (23,30–32),
– friendship:
  'the solemn communion of shining eyes' (25,26); 'They were lifted up: were friends.' (28,12),
– possession and power:
  "This belongs to us" (27,14), "All ours" (28,27), 'the right of domination.' (28,11–12)
But in contrast to the boys' romantic and innocent view, the following ambiguous incidents predict evil and destruction. Pushing a huge rock down a steep slope (26,8–31) seems to be an exciting game, a 'triumph' (26,30); but this also shows that innocent children are capable of releasing a destructive force: 'the forest further down shook as with the passage of an enraged monster.' (26,25–26) The rock is compared to 'a bomb' (26,28) that smashes 'a deep hole in the canopy of the forest.' (26,24) The image conveyed here is similar to that of the passenger tube which caused the scar in the jungle. This incident foreshadows future events and reveals a destructive force behind the children's innocent appearance. The image of a rock rolling down is repeated in the final part of the novel, when Roger dislodges a huge rock and kills Piggy.

It is also worth noting that the island is compared to a 'boat ... moving steadily astern.' (27,33) In view of later developments this metaphor may hint at the boys' regression to an inferior form of society in which violence and destruction prevail.

Another incident (29,7–30,5) shows that Jack is not able to kill 'because of the enormity of the knife descending and cutting into living flesh; because of the unbearable blood.' (29,30–32) Jack asserts, however, he will kill the pig the next time, 'there would be no mercy.' (30,2) The potential capability of destroying life is demonstrated here and becomes reality later.

Chapter 2: Fire on the Mountain

Summary Headlines

1. The second meeting starts in an organized way but ends in complete disorder. (31,1–37,22)
2. A signal fire is built, then lit. But it gets out of control and kills the young boy with the birthmark. (37,23–45,22)

Significance

1. The first attempt to establish some sort of democratic and parliamentary order fails.
2. The abrupt end to the meeting shows that the boys cannot stick to the rules they have agreed on.
3. The raging fire that kills one of the boys is symbolic of the destructive force generated by ignorance and irresponsibility.

Guides for Analysis

1. Compare the beginning and the end of this meeting.
2. Analyse Ralph's speech, Jack's struggle for power and the boys' reaction during the second assembly.
3. Identify the symbolic link between Piggy's glasses and the conch.
4. Consider the significance of the raging fire and the death of the young boy with the birthmark.

1. Compare the beginning and the end of this meeting.
   (31,1–18/36,29–37,22)

After the conch has been blown the meeting starts quietly. The boys are sitting around Ralph almost as if they were at an assembly. Ralph suggests making a signal fire for any ship that might come near the island. Electrified by this idea, the assembly breaks up immediately without anybody listening to further explanations. Everybody dashes to the top of the mountain. Jack claims the leadership: "Come on! Follow me!" (36,35) All the boys, including Ralph, follow Jack. Only Piggy views them with some contempt, commenting on their immature, mindless behaviour: "Like kids! ... Acting like a crowd of kids!" (37,8)

The rash end of the meeting (36,32–37,6) shows that the boys' version of parliamentary democracy is not working yet, because their spontaneous and irrational emotions are much stronger than their sense of reason and their understanding of social responsibility.

2. *Analyse Ralph's speech, Jack's struggle for power and the boys' reaction during the second assembly.* (31,1–37,22)

Ralph's speech is an example of his more or less unsuccessful attempts to focus the boys' attention on what is important for life on the island and for their rescue. Analysing his speech we find that besides his consistent line of argumentation, his spirit of adventure occasionally gets the better of him. (33,19–28)

At first he appears rather self-conscious and 'uncertain' (31,17), but as soon as he gives his report he becomes more self-confident, 'he could talk fluently and explain what he had to say.' (31,22–23)

Ralph describes the facts about their present situation:
– the island: "We're on an uninhabited island" (31,26)
– food: "There are pigs" (31,29)
– hunters: "We need hunters to get us meat" (32,1)
– responsibility: "There aren't any grown-ups. We shall have to look after ourselves." (32,4)

As a consequence, he points out that rules are needed to organize life on the island: "We can't have everybody talking at once. We'll have to have 'Hands up' like at school." (32,6–7) He puts emphasis on his personal authority: "I'll give the conch to the next person to speak ... he won't be interrupted. Except by me." (32,11–12/15)

Ralph defines the conch as a symbol of authority in their society and of the right to speak in the assembly. Initially, Ralph seems to convince the others by the strength of his arguments and by the logical conclusions he draws. But Jack keeps interrupting Ralph and disobeys the rules they agreed on. His exaggerated eagerness — "you need an army for hunting" (31,28), "Lots of rules! Then when anyone breaks 'em" (32,17) — betrays his priorities: hunting, intimidation, punishment, even violence. It also reveals the intensity of his desire for power and leadership.

It should be noted how the boys cope with fear and anxiety, which seem to be significant causes of their increasingly violent and aggressive behaviour. Whereas Ralph tries to reassure everybody that this is a "good island" (33,13) and that "we can have a good time" (33,19), one of the youngest boys, the boy with the birthmark, exhibits considerable distress and fear. He claims to have seen 'a beastie,' (34,24) 'a snake-thing' (34,20) that 'came in the dark' (35,1) and 'wanted to eat him.' (35,6)

Ralph argues that the boy's fears are simply 'nightmares' (35,11) and keeps repeating that "there isn't a beastie!" (35,16/19/27/32/35). But his rational explanation cannot convince the boys, who have now become frightened.

Jack for his part skilfully plays on the boys' fears and favours the idea that a beast might exist, in order to establish his own leadership and power, "if there was a snake we'd hunt it and kill it." (35,24–25)

Ralph, however, succeeds in lifting the boys' spirits again by pointing out that "we want to have fun. And we want to be rescued … and of course we shall be rescued." (36,10) The boys fully share Ralph's vain, almost childish hope that his father, the navy officer, will come and rescue them soon, because "the Queen has a big room full of maps and all the islands in the world are drawn there." (36,15–16) The boys are 'lifted towards safety by his words. They liked and now respected him.' (36,20–21)

Again this shows how easily the boys can be manipulated by irrational and rather naive arguments and how ignorant they are.

"We are made aware that innocence which consists largely of ignorance and irresponsibility may be far from harmless … . Irresponsibility and ignorance liberate a power that is more and more 'savage,' the 'squirrel' turns into a 'jaguar,' and that power appeals to something 'savage' in the boys themselves." (Kinkead-Weekes 27)

Therefore, the boys' psychological disposition seems to be just the right breeding ground for Jack's ambitious struggle for power and leadership.

3. Identify the symbolic link between Piggy's glasses and the conch. (39,2–41,14)

When the boys realize that they cannot light the fire, they feel embarrassed: 'Now the absurd situation was open …' (39,3–4) Then without asking Jack snatches Piggy's glasses from his face.

Piggy is frightened because he is almost blind without his glasses and he also fears that the conch might break: "I can hardly see! You'll break the conch!" (39,23–24)

The close connection between Piggy's glasses and the conch is significant for its symbolic value.

Piggy can see the situation on the island—symbolically through his glasses—quite rationally and clearly. His view contrasts with the romantic but fearful view held by the others. He understands what is needed for a civilized life and is concerned that the fragile conch, the instrument of order and authority, might break—which would eventually mean that civilized life on the island would come to an end.

In the final part of the novel (chapter 11) the murder of Piggy coincides with the breaking of the conch. The destruction of Piggy and the conch is also the defeat of democratic and civilized life and the starting point for unrestrained violence and terror.

4. Consider the significance of the raging fire and the death of the young boy with the birthmark. (42,12–45,22)

The fire gets out of control and explodes so that 'a quarter of a mile square of forest was savage with smoke and flame.' (43,7–8)

Stunned by the raging fire they have unleashed, the boys now listen to Piggy's warnings and his demands for more rational and responsible behaviour. "How can you expect to be rescued if you don't put first things first and act proper?" (44,7–8)

It is obvious that the fire has killed the young boy with the birthmark. Thus, the boys' fear of death has become reality. However, it was not the 'beast' that killed him, but the recklessness of those who had kindled the fire or, symbolically speaking, the 'beast' in them.

"What began as a playful cooperative effort to express the children's optimism and hope, and their belief in rescue, has inadvertently set free reckless, destructive, elemental forces." (Kaiser 29)

It should also be noted that the noise of the raging fire is compared to a 'drum-roll,' (45,21) which foreshadows the 'drum-roll' (189,16) of Ralph's intended execution in the final chapter. The tree that explodes in the fire 'like a bomb' (45,8) parallels the destruction of war in the world outside.

Thus, the raging fire and the death of the young boy can be interpreted both as a threat and as a call for critical self-awareness and social responsibility.

Chapter 3: Huts on the Beach

Summary Headlines

1. The different activities and preoccupations show the different interests and priorities of the boys. (46,1–53,14)
   - Jack wants to hunt and kill a pig,
   - Ralph and Simon are trying, unsuccessfully, to build shelters, which are necessary for survival,
   - most of the other boys prefer playing, swimming and eating fruit. At night, however, they are plagued by fears and nightmares.
2. Simon helps the little boy to find fruit and then retreats to a hiding place in the jungle in order to meditate. (53,15–55,16)

Significance

1. The boys' society is endangered due to differences of intention, irrational fears and by a growing conflict between Ralph and Jack.
2. The conflict between individuals is paralleled to the conflict between nations. How will the conflict be solved?
3. On the one hand the boys' fear of a beast mirrors the fear of evil that is part of human nature. On the other hand, human caring and social responsibility are illustrated by Simon's behaviour.

Guides for Analysis

1. Describe the growing conflict between Jack and Ralph and comment on its general significance.
2. What does Simon's behaviour reveal?

1. Describe the growing conflict between Jack and Ralph and comment on its general significance. (46,1–53,14)

Jack seems to degenerate into a state of primitive savagery, compelled 'to track down and kill.' (49,11) He is obsessed by hunting and killing a pig and behaves like an animal—'dog-like.' (46,7) When he misses the pig again, this determination to kill becomes even stronger, to the extent of 'swallowing him up.' (49,12)

Ralph and Simon are working hard to build shelters for the boys. Due to his sense of responsibility Ralph is well aware of the fact that shelter is needed, particularly for the little boys, in order to give them a feeling of protection, a sort of 'home.' (50,27)

According to Ralph, their only chance of rescue is by keeping the signal-fire burning. To Jack, however, hunting is more important than rescue: "Rescue? ... I'd like to catch a pig first." (51,14)

The relationship between Ralph and Jack is described as 'two continents of experience and feeling, unable to communicate.' (53,8–9) The antagonism intensifies, the conflict between the 'two continents' grows stronger.

Here the narrator parallels the conflict between individuals with the conflict between nations, thus providing the novel with a political dimension. Will the conflict be solved peacefully or will it develop into war?

2. What does Simon's behaviour reveal? (53,15–55,16)

The two parallel descriptions of Jack and Simon making their way through the jungle reveal a significant contrast. Simon's view of nature conveys a peaceful and joyful atmosphere. He senses 'the booming of a million bees at pasture,' (53,32) 'flowers and fruit ... on the same tree' (53,31) and 'a scent of ripeness' (53,32) 'aromatic bushes,' (54,18) a 'bowl of heat and light,' (54,18–19) 'gaudy butterflies' (54,30) and 'candle-like buds.' (55,6) When Simon moves on into the darkness of the jungle, he is not afraid, although 'he cocked a critical ear at the sounds of the island.' (54,31–32)

"Simon seems to be in solitary communion with nature, and in perfect peace." (Kaiser 32)

In contrast to Simon, Jack perceives nature quite differently. His attitude is marked by 'the oppressive silence' of the 'uncommunicative forest.' (46,23–24) Jack feels 'hunted.' (51,1)

Furthermore, Simon's sense of caring and responsibility is illustrated when he fetches fruit for the little boys and passes it 'back down to the endless, outstretched hands. When he had satisfied them he paused and looked round.' (54,4–6) This image conceivably resembles Jesus Christ distributing food to the five thousand:

"When Jesus emerged from his retreat he saw a vast crowd and was very deeply moved. ... He told the crowd to sit down on the grass. Then he took the five loaves and the two fish in his hands, and, looking up to Heaven, he thanked God, broke the loaves and passed them to his disciples who handed them to the crowd. Everybody ate and was satisfied." (Matthew 14, 14–21)

The religious image played upon here underlines Simon's altruism and social responsibility; but it also foreshadows his violent and tragic death. The significance of the biblical name, Simon, ties in with the religious imagery employed here.

Chapter 4: Painted Faces and Long Hair

Summary Headlines

1. The children's daily life alternates between enjoyment and fear. (56,1–57,25)
2. Some of the older boys start to smash the sand castles built by some of the younger boys and throw stones. (57,26–60,23)
3. Behind his mask of clay and charcoal Jack acquires a new identity. (60,24–62,12)
4. When a ship disappears over the horizon, a chance of rescue is lost. (62,13–66,16)
5. As the enmity between Ralph and Jack grows, the friendship between Ralph and Piggy becomes stronger. (66,17–73,11)

Significance

1. The metaphor of the children's daily life on the island suggests that the life of mankind starts full of hope but is eventually endangered by fear and menace.
2. The incident involving the smashing of sand castles and the stone throwing incident show how the individual's safety can be challenged by the aggressive behaviour of a few troublemakers.
3. Hiding behind the anonymity of a mask, Jack feels less inhibited about ignoring social and moral restraints.
4. Ralph's leadership gradually wanes. Jack's pig dance represents the new savage and aggressive tribe which replaces Ralph's organized, civilized and rational society.

Guides for Analysis

1. Comment on the metaphorical significance of the children's life on the island.
2. Why do some of the older boys smash sand castles and throw stones at the younger boys?
   How do the younger boys react? Comment on the significance of this incident.

3. Analyse the importance of Jack's mask.
4. Analyse the relationship between Ralph, Jack and Piggy.

1. Comment on the metaphorical significance of the children's life on the island. (56,1–57,25)

The children's daily routine starts joyfully in the morning. Then, at midday, 'strange things happen,' (56,11) and the sun even gazes down 'like an angry eye.' (56,21) At the close of the afternoon, the 'time of comparative coolness' (56,23) begins, 'menaced by the coming of the dark.' (56,23–24)

The coming darkness drops on the island 'like an extinguisher.' (56,25) And at night the boys' anticipation of menace and nightmares makes them extremely frightened and restless.

This chronology of emotions can be regarded as an extended metaphor of Golding's philosophy that life starts on a playful, optimistic note but can end in danger and trepidation.

"The passage holds the key to some of the story's deeper meaning. ... This is a story about young boys ... approaching the end of innocence. We see them young and playful at the beginning, and we will find them elderly in spirit by the end. The activity of the boys on an island is also a metaphor for the human race's struggle to survive." (Meitcke 39)

Furthermore, it should also be noted that due to the extreme living conditions, reality—as perceived by the boys—seems to dissolve and disintegrate. At night, the boys can no longer distinguish between reality and illusion, taking their fears and nightmares for reality.

2. Why do some of the older boys smash sand castles and throw stones at the younger boys?
   How do the younger boys react? Comment on the significance of this incident. (57,26–60,23)

Human life is endangered by people's violent and destructive behaviour. The victims and outsiders of any society are treated cruelly, almost sadistically. Some of the victims, however, even imitate this aggressive behaviour themselves in order to gain an 'illusion of mastery.' (59,18) This is illustrated in the following episode: (57,26–60,23).

While three of the little boys, Henry, Johnny and Percival enjoy building sand castles, the older boys, Roger and Maurice, come and destroy their creations. Maurice kicks sand into Percival's eyes and immediately hurries away, feeling the 'unease of wrong-doing.' (58,22) He is still aware of social control and a parent's 'heavy hand' (58,21) and recalls his punishment for a similar event 'in his other life.' (58,19)

This incident has a powerful influence on the 'innocent' (16,33) Johnny. He watches Percival with 'china-blue eyes' (58,30) and begins throwing sand at him—obviously imitating the aggressive behaviour he has just witnessed.

Thus, Percival becomes the victim of Maurice and Johnny. Johnny is left 'in triumphant possession of the castle ... throwing sand at an imaginary Percival.' (59,24–26) Percival—like Piggy—is treated as another outsider. He is a victim of the struggle for physical dominance over weaker members of a social group.

Meanwhile, although Roger throws stones at Henry, he is still aware of social norms, 'the taboos of the old life,' (60,12) and throws to miss. He has a sense of guilt and a bad conscience which are 'conditioned by civilization.' (60,14)

But "the restraint is only a taboo, a social conditioning or superstition, not anything innate." (Kinkead-Weekes 33)

Later Roger will throw stones and rocks to hurt and kill Piggy. Henry, who quite naively looks 'for the friend who was teasing him,' (60,20) enjoys 'control over living things' (59,15) and 'an illusion of mastery.' (59,18)

This episode reveals an increasing aggressiveness and violence which are still restrained, however, by social control. Considering the fact that the civilisation of the outside world is 'in ruins,' (60,15) an increasing tendency towards unrestricted violence and destruction is to be anticipated.

3. Analyse the importance of Jack's mask. (60,24–62,12)

The paint on Jack's face has different functions. It serves as dazzle paint 'like in the war' (61,11) for hunting pigs. It is absolutely necessary for Jack's new identity, behind which he can conceal his aggressiveness, 'liberated from shame and self-consciousness.' (62,3) Jack's development towards becoming an unscrupulous tyrant has begun.

4. Analyse the relationship between Ralph, Jack and Piggy. (62,13–73,11)

As the ship disappears over the horizon, Ralph and the other boys are left in despair. The chance of rescue is lost. Ralph's conviction that they would be rescued soon is shattered. He also feels betrayed by Jack, because he and his hunters have been more concerned with hunting than with keeping the fire burning. The growing conflict between Ralph and Jack escalates to open enmity between the two boys. Jack and his hunters appear from 'the unfriendly side of the mountain' (66,13) in a 'procession' (66,24)—similar to the first arrival of the choir boys. (17,31–18,16) They are chanting rhythmically and savagely "Kill the pig. Cut her throat. Spill her blood." (66,34)

Jack and his boys are excited by the 'enormity of ... cutting into living flesh.' (29,30–31) Jack reports about the "lashings of blood" (67,29) when cutting the pig's throat and is proud 'that they had outwitted a living thing, imposed their will upon it, taken away its life like a long satisfying drink.' (68,9–10)

Jack tries to conceal his 'thirst for blood,' arguing that they have to kill because they need the meat. (69,5) When Ralph accuses Jack of irresponsible behaviour, Jack threatens him with the bloodied knife.

Jack, who is extremely frustrated and irritated by Ralph's accusations, does not dare to attack him, because he is uncertain as to whether the boys would support him. For the time being, he finds an outlet for his aggressiveness by turning to Piggy and hitting him viciously. The breaking of one of Piggy's lenses is symbolic of the partial removal of clear-sighted rationality in the boys' society.

As the enmity between Ralph and Jack intensifies, a friendship between Ralph and Piggy develops. 'Not even Ralph knew how a link between him and Jack had been snapped and fastened elsewhere.' (71,5–6) Ralph's attitude towards Piggy has changed considerably in comparison with Ralph's earlier opinion that Piggy 'was a bore,' that 'his fat, ass-mar and his matter-of-fact ideas were dull.' (63,3–4) Now he starts to appreciate Piggy's rationality and social responsibility as being integral parts of democratic, peaceful and civilized life.

Ralph is concerned about the regression to social irresponsibility, primitive ritual and savagery and calls a meeting in the hope of restoring civilized order to the island, fully aware of Jack's increasing authoritarian control over the boys.

Chapter 5: Beast from Water

Summary Headlines

1. In calling an assembly Ralph wants to re-establish his leadership, to restore a civilized life on the island and to remind the boys of the essential rules. (74,1–76,14)
2. The third assembly begins as a hopeful attempt to reorganize the boys' lives but ends in chaos with Jack taking the lead. (76,15–89,8)
3. Ralph, Piggy and Simon are left behind, quite helpless and idealizing the adult world. (89,9–91,24)

Significance

1. The assembly shows that reason has failed, fear dominates, irrationality is on the increase and savagery is rearing its ugly head.
2. The boys' irrational belief that some beast might exist and threaten them produces fear and anxiety that lead, ultimately, to the disintegration of their society.
3. The beast, however, is not some kind of animal or alien but stands for the dark and evil side of human nature.

Guides for Analysis

1. What does Ralph want to achieve in the third assembly?
2. Analyse the development of the third meeting and comment on its significance.
3. Describe Ralph's, Piggy's and Simon's situation after the assembly.

1. What does Ralph want to achieve in the third assembly? (74,1–76,14)

In calling an assembly, Ralph wants to re-establish his leadership, restore civilized life on the island and remind the boys of the rules according to which they must live.

From his recent experiences Ralph has become more sensitive to the difficult situation on the island, 'the wearisomeness of this life' (74,6) which contrasts with his 'first enthusiastic exploration' (74,9) on the island. Now he discovers 'dirt and decay' (74,24) and is worried that this meeting might end up in a complete mess. But he is determined that 'this meeting must not be fun, but business.' (74,17)

2. Analyse the development of the third meeting and comment on its significance. (76,15–89,8)

The third assembly begins as a hopeful attempt to reorganize life on the island but instead creates further chaos and finally culminates in complete disorder.

The assembly starts late in the afternoon and ends at night—that is, metaphorically speaking, in complete darkness, shifting from reason to irrationality.

Ralph wants "to put things straight," (77,4–5/8) focusing as he does on the main problems:
– a fresh water supply (77,15–24),
– the unfinished shelters (77,26–35),
– the toilet problem (77,37–78,17),
– the signal fire for rescue (78,18–79,12) and
– the boys' irrational fears (79,27–80,6).

Ralph reiterates his worries about the boys' increasing irrationality: "Things are breaking up. I don't understand why. We began well; we were happy. And then—." (79,29–30) He wants the boys to make a new start and "be happy." (80,6) He argues that fire and rescue are their only hope and tries to rationalize their fears—"there's nothing in it." (80,2)

In contrast to Ralph, Jack sees fear as a bad dream they have to cope with, "as for the fear—you'll have to put up with that like the rest of us." (80,15–16) He adds that "there is no beast in the forest" (81,2–3) but adds to the boys' fears by mentioning "a dark thing, a beast" (80,26) which he would hunt and kill. In order to emphasize his point he asks the rhetorical questions: "Am I a hunter or am I not?" (80,35)

Thus, Jack plays on the boys' superstitious fears, exploiting them in his endeavour to become the leader.

Piggy meanwhile argues that "life is scientific" (81,27–28) and "if there's something wrong, there's something to put it right." (81,15–16) Supporting Ralph, Piggy reassures the boys that there is no reason to be afraid of anything. With Jack in mind, Piggy adds that fear can only be caused by real people, "we get frightened of people." (81,36) He believes that a person like Jack can implant fear in other people's hearts through violence, aggression and terrorism.

Phil, Percival and Maurice claim to have seen "something moving among the trees, something big and horrid," (82,20/27) a beast coming "out of the sea," (85,18) animals in the sea "that have not been found yet" (85,24) or "some sort of ghost." (87,4)

Simon tries unsuccessfully to 'express mankind's essential illness' (86,28–29) and remarks that "maybe there is a beast ... maybe it's only us." (86,12/24)

It is Simon "who gropes to a recognition that the fear leading to the disintegration of their world is finally not external to them, but ingrained in themselves." (Wilson 26)

Here the philosophy of Golding's novel is put in a nutshell: the beast is not some sort of animal threatening people but signifies a dark and evil side of human nature present in every human being.

And it is Jack who embodies this evil side. He openly disregards the conch, and in so doing breaks the most important democratic rule. He assaults Piggy and shows his contempt for order and social rules: "Who cares," (88,34) "Bollocks to the rules." (89,1) Jack succeeds in breaking up the assembly, driving the mass into a state of frenzy: "If there's a beast, we'll hunt it down! We'll close in and beat and beat and beat—!" (89,1–2)

The outcome of the assembly is that reason fails, fear predominates, irrationality increases and savagery develops.

3. Describe Ralph's, Piggy's and Simon's situation after the assembly. (89,9–91,24)

The three boys are left behind helpless like "three blind mice." (90,11) Ralph is completely desperate, willing even to give up his leadership. He even questions Piggy about the existence of "ghosts ... or beasts?" (89,26)

Piggy draws comfort from his idealized image of an adult world which appears to him peaceful and reasonable. "Grown-ups know things ... They ain't afraid of the dark. They'd meet and have tea and discuss. Then things 'ud be all right." (91,7–9) The three boys long for a hopeful message from the adult world—"If only they could send us something grown-up ... a sign or something.". (91,17–18)

When the boys talk in the dark, trying 'to convey the majesty of adult life,' (91,12–13) the implied irony should be noted. The adult world is at war and 'in ruins,' (60,15) and not as peaceful and reasonable as the boys assume.

Chapter 6: Beast from Air

Summary Headlines

1. A pilot shot down in an air battle falls down onto the mountain top and in the boys' view becomes the beast from the air. (92,1–93,6)
2. Sam and Eric, who are frightened by the noise and shadows made by the parachute of the dead pilot, give an exaggerated account of the beast. Horror and fear spread. (93,7–99,13)
3. After a controversial debate, an expedition is organized to search for the beast. (99,14–105,6)

Significance

1. The boys' life on the island reflects and parallels life in the world at large. Human standards are abandoned, mankind regresses to violence and terror. The 'majesty of adult life' is a delusion.
2. The boys' perception of reality is distorted by fear and anxiety. Fearful illusions are taken for reality.
3. The expedition signifies the beginning of an exploration for the evil and destructive side of nature and of mankind.

Guides for Analysis

1. What does the sign from the adult world suggest?
2. How do the boys perceive reality?
3. What does the fourth assembly show?
4. Analyse the significance of the expedition to the inhospitable part of the island.

1. What does the sign from the adult world suggest? (92,1–93,6)

An ironical response to the boys' hope of a sign from the 'majesty of adult life' (91,13) is given at the beginning of this chapter. It shows that the 'majesty of adult life' is a delusion. An airman shot down in a battle 'fought at ten miles height,' (92,12–13), drops onto the mountain top and becomes the Beast from Air. This sign reveals that the world is dominated by war, inhumanity and violence—and not by hope and rescue. Humane standards are abandoned, mankind regresses to savagery.

"The parachutist shows man's inhumanity to man, the record of what human beings have done to one another throughout human history. The children are revealing the same nature as the grown-ups ... . The child world is only a microcosm of the adult world." (Kinkead-Weekes 38)

"Golding himself has commented that the dead airman, riddled with bullets, is an image of history; a reminder of man's unremitting aggression against man." (Wilson 28)

2. How do the boys perceive reality? (93,7–97,19)

The boys' perception of reality is affected by fear, anxiety and a fearful imagination. Sam and Eric, for example, interpret the 'plopping noise of fabric blown open' (95,8–9)—i.e. the dangling movements of the dead parachutist caught up in strings—as a mysterious and horrifying beast.

Their exaggerated report becomes a horror story of a winged monster, all teeth and claws, that has pursued them down the mountain, that "nearly touched me" (97,10)—"Am I bleeding?" (97,15)

Horror and fear immediately spread to all the other boys as Sam and Eric relate what they have seen. Even Ralph and Piggy are affected by the terrifying story. 'Soon the darkness was full of claws, full of the awful unknown and menace.' (96,4–5) The boys' imaginations produce nightmares that are taken for reality.

3. What does the fourth assembly show? (97,20–99,13)

During the fourth assembly the fierce hostility between Ralph and Jack and their struggle for power and leadership continue. Ralph is concerned about the signal fire as a means of rescue and shows a great sense of responsibility for the younger boys, "someone's got to look after them." (98,4)

Jack on the other hand does not care about the younger children—"Sucks to the littluns." (98,3) He challenges the authority of Ralph and the conch—"We don't need the conch any more" (98,23)—his only concern being his lust for power, hunting and killing. "This'll be a real hunt!" (97,21)

4. Analyse the significance of the expedition to the inhospitable part
of the island. (99,14—105,6)

The second expedition parallels the first—"Do you remember?"
(103,1)—but is in fact quite different.

Whereas the first expedition that led to the mountain-top is characterized by enjoyment and happiness, the second is dominated by fearful
undertones like 'personal hell,' (100,17) 'the breathing of some stupen-
dous creature' (101,33) and 'the sleeping leviathan,' (102,2) an obvious
allusion to the political philosophy of Thomas Hobbes (see 201—202).

This expedition leads to the other side of the island, 'the pink bastion,'
(100,34) in Ralph's view "a rotten place." (102,33)

This side of the island is already described in the first chapter: 'There
... was another island; a rock ... standing like a fort, facing them ...
with one bold, pink bastion.' (27,19—21) In their search for the beast, the
boys are beginning to explore the threatening, menacing and dark side of
human nature. Simon is the only one who does not believe in the existence of the beast, but sees 'the picture of a human at once heroic and
sick' (100,2—3)—resembling the corpse of the dead airman.

The metaphor suggests that humanity is falling apart, degenerating
into violence, destruction and war. Simon's view of humanity might also
be related to Jack, who is heroic but sick with lust for power, hunting
and killing.

At the end of this chapter, the boys' enjoyment of rolling rocks recalls
a similar incident in chapter one (26,8—31). Jack's threatening remark—
"Shove a palm trunk under that (rock) and if an enemy came—"
(103,4)—foreshadows cruel events, preparing for the murder of Piggy
who will be killed by a rock.

Thus the expedition to the inhospitable part of the island metaphorically suggests the discovery of the evil and destructive side of nature and
of mankind, 'the darkness of man's heart.' (193,29)

Chapter 7: Shadows and Tall Trees

Summary Headlines

1. Ralph is aware of the depressing circumstances on the island and finds comfort in daydreaming of his secure and peaceful home. Simon assures him that he will return home. (106,1–109,26)
2. When a boar breaks cover, Ralph throws his stick at the animal and feels proud afterwards. (109,27–111,8)
3. A mock hunt with Robert playing a pig nearly gets out of control. (111,9–112,16)
4. The boys search for the beast, and when they come to the dead pilot on top of the mountain, Ralph takes the bulging parachute for the beast. The boys flee in complete horror. (112,17–120,7)

Significance

1. The reality of the depressing situation on the island is contrasted with the illusion of a peaceful and secure home. In his daydreams Ralph escapes from reality.
2. The mock hunt reveals that games, pretence and cruel reality can hardly be distinguished and that a potential desire to hurt and kill can no longer be resisted.
3. The search for the beast emphasizes the message that irrational decisions and actions are made on the basis of hostility, hate, fear and the challenge to demonstrate courage.

Guides for Analysis

1. Analyse the contrast between illusion and reality.
2. What experience does Ralph make and what does he realize about himself?
3. What does the search for the beast reveal?

1. Analyse the contrast between illusion and reality. (106,1–109,26)

Ralph's daydreaming contrasts significantly with the situation he is confronted with. Aware of his dirty appearance, Ralph considers the depressing circumstances on the island. He realizes the disgust he feels at the outer and inner deterioration of the boys. 'With the memory of his sometimes clean self as a standard' (100,26–27) he feels helpless. His habit of biting his fingernails is indicative of a regression to early childhood – "Be sucking my thumb next." (106,22)

In his daydreams Ralph escapes from reality. He remembers his childhood paradise at home, the 'wild ponies,' (109,5) the 'bowl of cornflakes with sugar and cream' (109,13–14) and his favourite books 'on the shelf by the bed.' (109,14) Ralph remembers the days when everything was secure, 'good-humoured and friendly,' (109,26) when 'you could go indoors when you were cold and look out of the window.' (109,10–11) Simon seems to understand Ralph's thoughts and assures him that "you'll get back." (108,4/11/20) Simon appears to be like a prophet – 'kneeling on one knee, looking down from a higher rock.' (108,5–6) But Simon does not say 'we'll get back', perhaps prophetically presaging his own coming death.

2. What experience does Ralph make and what does he get to know about himself? (109,27–112,16)

Ralph's peaceful world of daydreams is suddenly interrupted by reality. When a boar breaks cover, Ralph immediately throws his stick at the animal and is 'full of fright and apprehension and pride.' (110,8–9) He is proud of having wounded the animal and for the first time identifies with the hunters. Ralph feels that 'hunting was good after all' (110, 21–22) and 'sunned himself in their new respect.' (110,21) This shows that he still feels dependent on the admiration and respect of the group, which is important for his self-confidence. He wants to be part of the group – not an outsider.

The boys become excited by the talk of killing. During the ensuing mock hunt with Robert playing a pig, Ralph grabs at Robert's 'brown, vulnerable flesh.' (111,27–28) When the game nearly gets out of control, Robert struggles for his life and squeals 'in mock terror, then in real pain.' (111,14–15) In this scene Ralph feels a 'sudden thick excitement' (111,19–20) and the 'desire to squeeze and hurt.' (111,28)

In contrast to Ralph's peaceful world of daydreams, this episode reveals a darker and destructive side to Ralph's character: the potential desire to hurt and kill. Like the other boys, Ralph is in danger of being attracted to and then overwhelmed by instincts of aggression, violence and destruction.

After the mock hunt Ralph's reaction—'"Just a game," said Ralph uneasily' (112,2)—reveals that he has learnt something about himself hitherto unknown to him.

According to Jack, the mock hunt "was a good game." (112,1)

But the "line between game, pretence and reality is becoming much more difficult to draw." (Kinkead-Weekes 49)

Robert, the victim, who has struggled for his life, points out Jack's desire to destroy and kill: "You want a real pig ... because you've got to kill him." (112,14−15) Jack can hardly resist the urge to destroy life. 'Jack had him (Robert) by the hair and was brandishing his knife.' (111,23)

3. What does the search for the beast reveal? (112,17−120,7)

The search for the beast emphasizes the fact that
− the hostility between Ralph and Jack is getting stronger,
− responsibility, reason and logical thought are abandoned,
− irrational decisions are made on the grounds of rivalry, hostility and hate for each other,
− the challenge to show courage is a strong motivation for the boys.
As the search for the beast continues, Ralph becomes aware of 'the rising antagonism' (115,1) between himself and Jack, a clash of emotions which is described as a 'fresh rub of two spirits in the dark.' (116,14)

Ralph is aware of his responsibility for the boys they have left behind, but he now seems determined to compete with Jack, who provokes him with cynical and scornful remarks: "We mustn't let anything happen to Piggy, must we?" (114,8) "Would you rather go back to the shelters and tell Piggy?" (115,7) "If you're frightened of course−." (115,26)

Ralph is aware that an expedition in the darkness would make no sense at all. The text clearly illustrates the boys' irrational decision to climb the mountain and search for the beast:
− "We're silly." (116,27)
− 'The darkness seemed to flow round them like a tide.' (116,34−35)
− 'Ralph's eyes were blinded with tears.' (116,36−37)
− 'small devils of dust' (117,2−3)
− 'he coughed to remember how silly they were.' (117,3−4)

- "We're being fools." (117,8)
- 'The sting of ashes in his eyes, tiredness, fear, enraged him.' (117,15–16)
- 'this mad expedition' (117,30)

"Their journey is like a negative repeat of that joyful first exploration of the island ... They go in darkness, out of dread and full of hate for each other". (Meitcke 60)

When Jack tells the others what he saw—"I saw a thing on top ... bulge on the mountain." (118,5/10)—Ralph feels challenged to exhibit 'bravado.' (118,9) He obviously wants to impress the others and suggests they "go and look." (118,20) Ralph's senses, his reason and clear-sightedness are blurred, 'Green light of nausea appeared ...' (119,15) 'Ashes blew into Ralph's face from the dead fire. He could not see ... and the top of the mountain was sliding sideways.' (119,19–21) His distorted perception of reality is due to the extreme mental strain resulting from his fear. Seeing a 'rock-like hump,' (119,30) Ralph 'bound himself together with his will, fused his fear and loathing into hatred, and stood up.' (119,32–34)

The corpse of the dead parachutist appears like 'a great ape ... sitting asleep with its head between its knees. Then the wind roared in the forest, there was confusion in the darkness and the creature lifted its head, holding towards them the ruin of a face.' (119,36–120,3)

Chapter 8: Gift for the Darkness

Summary Headlines

1. The boys describe the beast in a wildly exaggerated, fearful and boasting manner. (121,1–122,6)
2. Jack fails in his challenge to Ralph's leadership, sobs with humiliation and runs away. (122,7–124,18)
3. Simon suggests returning to the top of the hill to find out what makes them afraid. When the fire is lit at a new place, Ralph and Piggy notice that some of the boys have left to follow Jack. (124,19–128,34)
4. A pig is slaughtered by Jack and his hunters in a particularly cruel way. The sow's head is placed on a stick and left as a gift to placate the beast. (128,35–133,4)
5. Simon encounters the grinning head of the dead pig, 'the Lord of the Flies'. It seems as if the Lord of the Flies is talking to him, warning and threatening him that the beast is part of everybody. (133,5–36/138,6– 139,17)
6. Ralph and Piggy wonder why things have gone wrong. Jack's group raids them for fire and then invites them to share the pig-meat and the nocturnal fun on Castle Rock. (134,1–138,5)

Significance

1. Intrigued by the 'fun, games and meat' some of the boys feel inclined to follow—first secretly, then openly.
2. The brutal killing of the sow shows that the powers of terror and destruction personified by Jack triumph over the restraints of civilization and the values represented by Ralph.
3. Ralph's crucial question, "What makes things break up like they do?" is answered by Simon's encounter with the Lord of the Flies. Evil, hate, violence, terror—the beast—are part of the human condition and are responsible for destruction, hate and war.

Guides for Analysis

1. What does the boys' account of the beast show?
2. Explain Jack's intention when blowing the conch and calling an assembly.
3. Comment on the boys' evaluation of the new situation they are confronted with.
4. Analyse the significance of the slaughter of the pig.
5. Analyse Simon's encounter with the Lord of the Flies and explain why 'things break up like they do.'

1. What does the boys' account of the beast show? (121,1–122,6)

The boys' account of 'the beast' is a wildly exaggerated and fearful interpretation of what they imagine they saw. Reason, clear-sightedness and rationality are on the wane.

Golding's narrative technique

"shows us things not as they might appear to a neutral observer, but as they are coloured and shaped by the hopes, fears and other emotions of the boys themselves." (Wilson 33)

Ralph has almost given up hope of rescue, because—ironically —"that thing squats by the fire as though it didn't want us to be rescued." (121,29) The original fireplace meant hope of rescue, now it means fear and menace.

2. Explain Jack's intention when blowing the conch and calling an assembly. (122,7–124,18)

It is Jack who blows the conch to call an assembly. He openly challenges Ralph's position as leader. But Jack misjudges the situation, and his attempt to overthrow Ralph as leader fails. Humiliated and infuriated like a frustrated little boy, Jack cries helplessly, "I'm not going to play any longer. Not with you." (124,3)

Jack turns his back on the parliamentary assembly to establish his own totalitarian society. And boys like Roger and Maurice, who are attracted by the fun and games on offer, soon leave secretly to join him.

"Jack leaves the parliamentary triangle never to return to it, and disappears over the white sand into the darkness of the forest. The orderly grouping of the platform triangle will soon be replaced by the revolving movement of the tribal circle." (Kaiser 48)

3. *Comment on the boys' evaluation of the new situation they are confronted with.* (124,19–128,34)

The boys react in various ways to the new situation.

Ralph feels depressed and pessimistic — "no help ... nothing to be done." (124,32) Piggy, who is 'so full of delight and expanding liberty in Jack's departure' (126,7–8) suggests building a new fire near the platform and thus counterbalances Ralph's despair.

The omniscient narrator comments on Piggy's pragmatic suggestion with subtle irony: 'intellecutal daring,' (125,31) 'the greatest ideas are the simplest.' (126,6)

Piggy does not recognize the logic in Simon's suggestion to climb the mountain and find what makes them afraid. It should now be the boys' first priority to inquire into the circumstances of their fear. But the 'circle shivered with dread' (125,6) and even Piggy looks at Simon with an 'expression of derisive incomprehension.' (125,7). In Piggy's view, Simon is "cracked" (128,23) and should not be taken seriously.

When Simon climbs the mountain to look for the 'thing' he kneels down and 'the arrow of sun' (128,29) falls on him. The description conveys religious or metaphysical connotations suggestive of forthcoming dramatic revelations.

4. *Analyse the significance of the slaughter of the pig.* (128,35–133,4)

The slaughter of the pig reveals the deliberate cruelty and brutality of Jack's increasingly savage tribe.

Jack is 'brilliantly happy' (128,36) when he is standing in front of his group of boys, who wear the 'remains of a black cap' (129,1–2) and whose voices 'ages ago ... had been the song of angels.' (129,2–3) The narrator's comment reminds the reader of the previous innocence of the choir boys.

Jack leads his obedient hunters to a large sow 'sunk in deep maternal bliss ... fringed with a row of piglets.' (130,1–3)

Jack's decision to destroy this peaceful and idyllic gathering betrays the extent to which he has committed himself to the evil and cruel side of human nature. The bloody slaughtering is described in terms of a brutal rape: the hunters are 'wedded to her in lust, excited by the long chase and the dropped blood' (130, 34–35) and then 'the sow collapsed under them ... they were heavy and fulfilled upon her.' (131,14–15)

Jack and his boys no longer have any social and moral restraints and degenerate into brutal sadists revelling in torture, terror and killing.

The powers of destruction represented by Jack triumph over the restraints of social, human and moral values represented by Ralph.

5. Analyse Simon's encounter with the Lord of the Flies and explain why 'things break up like they do.'

Simon's encounter with the Lord of the Flies (133,5–36/138,6–139,17) is interrupted and paralleled with a passage (134,1–138,5) that illustrates
– Ralph's depression and resignation,
– his increasing dependence on Piggy,
– Piggy's pride at being accepted by Ralph and
– Jack's raid for fire.
Ralph's crucial question—"what makes things break up like they do?" (135,16)—is answered by Simon following his encounter with the Lord of the Flies.

From his hide-out Simon has witnessed the killing of the sow. When the hunters escape in fear of the spiked pig's head, Simon approaches and registers the flies on the pig's guts, body and head. Then Simon projects his own thoughts—and Golding's philosophy—onto the pig's head, whose eyes are 'dim with the infinite cynicism of adult life.' (133,7–8) This contrasts significantly with the earlier belief in 'the majesty of adult life.'(91,13) Simon realizes 'the gaze,' (133,35) on the pig's head, 'held by that ancient, inescapable recognition,' (133,35) denoting how destructive and evil forces are part of human beings and lead to things breaking up.

The philosophy of the message is illustrated in the corresponding scenes.

Firstly, Ralph is worried about the loss of social responsibility—"Supposing I got like the others—not caring. What'ud become of us?" (135,7–8) What's more, he doubts whether rationality, social responsibility and human values still matter.

Secondly, Jack and his boys appear like 'demoniac figures,' (135,25) when raiding Ralph and his boys for fire. In this context Jack is described as being 'safe from shame or self-consciousness behind the mask of his paint.' (135,38–136,1) He proudly demonstrates his new status as dictator, "Chief." (136,18)

Thirdly, even Ralph and Piggy seem to be attracted by Jack's promise of having meat and fun. Thus, they join Jack's tribe and in a savage ritual participate in Simon's murder.

During his encounter with the Lord of the Flies Simon recognizes that the beast is not some creature from outside. It is the destructive and evil part of human beings—"I'm part of you" (138,26)—which is metaphorically embodied in the Lord of the Flies. The term is a translation of the Hebrew word 'Beelzebub,' another name for Satan or the devil. The Lord of the Flies thus stands for evil, hate, violence, savagery, terror and murder—the beast inherent in man, which is responsible for destruction and war, "why it's no go? Why things are what they are?" (138,26–27)

Simon recognizes that the beast is also present in the savage behaviour of Jack's tribe, "you'll only meet me down there." (139,1–2) The phrase "we shall do you" (139,14) is even more menacing and suggests that the boys—including even Ralph and Piggy—might kill Simon.

Chapter 9: A View to a Death

Summary Headlines

1. Simon discovers the dead pilot on the hilltop, frees the parachute lines and wants to tell the other boys that 'the beast' is harmless. (140,1–142,4)
2. Ralph and Piggy realize that a number of boys have left them in order to join Jack's tribe. (142,5–143,9)
3. Jack appears like a dictator and invites all the boys to join his tribe. (143,10–145,29)
4. When a heavy thunderstorm breaks out, Jack commands the boys to begin their ritual dance and chant, which drives them into a hysterical frenzy. (145,30–147,2)
5. Simon, who wants to tell the boys about his discovery, is taken for the beast and killed by a mad and violent crowd. When the body of the parachutist is blown into the lagoon by the storm, the boys rush screaming into the darkness. (147,2–147,31)
6. Simon's broken body is washed out to sea. (147,32–148,30)

Significance

1. Simon's discovery of the truth confirms his earlier belief that the beast is an illusion generated by the boys' fear and imagination. Whereas the beast on the hilltop no longer exists, it still becomes part of the savage crowd.
2. All the boys, even Ralph and Piggy, take part in the murder of Simon and are guilty of his death. This emphasizes that the potential for violence, destruction and crime exists in every human being.
3. Jack has won the struggle for leadership and has become more or less a dictator of a totalitarian society based on greed and selfishness. It offers meat and fun—but not rescue.
4. Nature's response to the dramatic events serves as a metaphorical comment on the behaviour of the mindless crowd, the cruel and violent people and the suffering victim.

Guides for Analysis

1. What does Simon discover?
2. Analyse the more general significance of Jack's appearance.
3. Comment on the parallel between the dramatic events and natural phenomena.
4. Why is Simon killed?
5. Analyse the significance of the final part of this chapter.

1. What does Simon discover? (140,1–142,4)

When Simon discovers the corpse of the parachutist, he realizes 'the mechanics of this parody' (141,21–22) and that 'the beast was harmless and horrible.' (142,1) This confirms his earlier intuition that the beast from outside is an illusion generated by the boys' fears and imaginations.

Therefore, he is determined to assure the boys that there is no reason for fear or superstition and—out of concern for the boys—he decides that 'the news must reach the others as soon as possible.' (142,1–2)

The description of Simon staggering down the mountain to the boys—'his legs gave beneath him' (142,3)—reveals his great effort to relieve them of their fear.

Tragically, nobody wants to listen to Simon's discovery of the truth.

2. Analyse the more general significance of Jack's appearance. (142,5–145,33)

Jack appears as an embodiment of authoritarian power and dictatorship. He is masked as a tribal chief, enthroned, 'painted and garlanded ... like an idol.' (143,23–24). He shouts commands like "take them some meat," (144,8) "give me a drink" (144,29) and, almost threateningly: "Has everybody eaten as much as they want?" (144,13/18) The narrator comments on his tone as 'a warning given out of the pride of ownership.' (144,19)

Jack does not care about democratic rules or the conch, once a symbol of civilized and democratic order; "the conch doesn't count at this end of the island." (145,18)

The omniscient narrator observes ironically that Jack's power 'lay in the brown swell of his forearms; authority sat on his shoulder and chattered in his ear like an ape.' (144,31–32)

Jack has finally become a brutal and mindless dictator. Piggy's earlier question—"What are we? Humans? Or animals? Or savages?" (88,15)—is obviously answered here.

3. Comment on the parallel between the dramatic events and natural phenomena.

Heat and humidity build up to a tropical thunderstorm. 'Between the flashes of lightning the air was dark and terrible.' (146,11–12) This parallels the rising tension of the action.

Since he cannot provide shelter for the boys, who run about screaming with fear, Jack realizes that he might relinquish his power to Ralph but evades Ralph's challenging demand—"Where are your shelters? What are you going to do about that?" (146,1–2) Jack commands the boys to start their ritual dance instead—thus effectively distracting the group. Even Ralph and Piggy, fearing the isolation of staying outside, join the circle and become part of 'the throb and stamp of a single organism.' (146,27)

'Piggy and Ralph, under the threat of the sky, found themselves eager to take place in this demented but partly secure society. They were glad to touch the brown backs of the fence that hemmed in the terror and made it governable.' (146,16–20) The chant—"Kill the beast! Cut his throat! Spill his blood!" (146,21)—sends them into a hysterical frenzy, a state paralleled by the response of nature. 'The dark sky was shattered by a blue-white scar. An instant later the noise was on them like the blow of a gigantic whip. The chant rose a tone in agony.' (146,28–30)

4. Why is Simon killed?

In mass madness the hysterical and violent crowd takes Simon for the beast and kills him. The boys 'leapt on to the beast, screamed, struck, bit, tore. There were no words, and no movements but the tearing of teeth and claws.' (147,16–18)

The murderous circle is described as 'the mouth' (147,11) that 'crunched and screamed.' (147,11) The vicious crowd has finally become a voracious, predatory animal—'the beast' itself.

"It is profoundly ironic that Simon, who is essentially a visionary and 'saint', should be mistaken for the Beast by the Beast itself, which is the mob violence of his destroyers." (Wilson 80)

Simon, the victim, is kneeling in the centre of the circle with his 'arms folded' (147,12) over his face like a martyr.

Simon is unable to bring the message about 'a dead man on a hill' (147,9) to the others, because his voice of reason and humanity is drowned by the hysteria and mindlessness of the crowd. The 'dead man on a hill' is of course the pilot but this phrase also suggests a religious connotation: Jesus Christ's crucifixion.

When the dead pilot is carried out to the sea by a strong wind, it is obvious that 'the beast' on top of the hill no longer exists. Now, the savage crowd has itself become the beast or—as Golding puts it—"the only enemy of man is inside him." (200,11)

It is significant that even Ralph and Piggy take part in the murder of Simon. Before, they had tried to stop the destructive tendencies in Jack but now, even they join in the ritual which leads to Simon's death.

In this passage Golding seeks to point out man's innate desire to torture and kill. Golding has explained his intentions precisely:

"I am thinking of the vileness beyond all words that went on, year after year, in the totalitarian states. ... I believed that the condition of man was to be a morally diseased creation and that the best job I could do at the time, was to trace the connection between his diseased nature and the international mess he gets himself into." (198,24–25/199,4–7)

5. *Analyse the significance of the final part of this chapter.*
   (147,32–148,30)

In the final, enigmatic part of this chapter, nature responds to 'the beast ... huddled on the pale beach' (148,3) with light and brightness:
– 'lamps of stars' (147,33)
– 'a streak of phosphorescence' (148,5)
– 'clear sky' (148,7)
– 'angular bright constellations' (148,7)
– 'advancing clearness' (148,11) and
– 'brightness' (148,18).
The imagery of light and brightness in connection with Simon's dead and broken body conveys a poetic, almost metaphysical and transcendental message. The reference to the earth as just being part of the whole universe 'the film of water on the earth planet' (148,25), further demonstrates the insignificance of the earth in relation to the rest of the universe.

The contrasting perspectives of little 'inquisitive bright creatures'

(148,28) and the cosmic 'angular bright ... steadfast constellations' (148,7/29) show how small and insignificant man's endeavours on earth are.

'The water ... dressed Simon's coarse hair with brightness. The line of his cheek silvered and the turn of his shoulder became sculptured marble.' (148,17–19) This description further emphasizes Simon's role as martyr. Nature pays tribute to a martyr who has discovered the truth and is killed by his ignorant fellow people.

The 'advancing clearness' (148,11) signifies the gradual emergence of Simon's discovery, which ironically and tragically has not reached the others yet.

Chapter 10: The Shell and the Glasses

Summary Headlines

1. Ralph admits his guilt in taking part in the murder of Simon. Piggy deceives himself and finds excuses. (149,1– 152,26)
2. At Castle Rock Jack wields his absolute power. Wilfred is beaten and tied up, the fears of the beast are again raised. (152,27–155,28)
3. In a fierce attack on Ralph's shelters Jack steals Piggy's glasses. (155,29–162,9)

Significance

1. Piggy's rational clear-sightedness is losing ground, self-deception is growing stronger.
2. Jack, the dictator, exercises his authoritarian power in a threatening and menacing way in order to intimidate the others and to establish his regime even further.
3. Roger becomes an unscrupulous executioner who wields cruel punishment on dissidents.
4. In stealing Piggy's glasses, the symbol of rescue, rational vision and security, Jack completes his acquisition of absolute power.

Guides for Analysis

1. Explain the strategy of self-deception illustrated in the first part of the chapter.
2. What strategies does Jack employ to keep his followers under control?
3. Comment on the significance of Roger's 'illumination.'
4. Why does Jack steal Piggy's glasses?

1. Explain the strategy of self-deception illustrated in the first part of the chapter. (149,1–152,26)

Self-deception is the only reaction left when people cannot face reality any longer or are unable to cope with their guilt and lack of responsibility.

Ralph knows that they have killed Simon. He is deeply worried and admits his guilt for taking part in the murder: "That was murder," (150,20) "The things we did," (150,34) "All of us!" (151,23)

Ralph accepts his responsibility. He is frightened 'of us' (151,16) and begins to understand Simon's message of humanity's essential disease, the existence of a destructive force in every human being.

Piggy, however, tries to dismiss and rationalize what they have done. He finds excuses and claims to have "done nothing ... seen nothing." (151,29–30) He searches for a self-deceiving 'formula' (150,30) that puts the blame on the thunderstorm and on the victim himself, "he had no business crawling like that out of the dark. He was batty. He asked for it." (151,10–12)

Ralph finally agrees with Piggy's self-deceiving excuse that they were only "on the outside" (151,29) of the murder. The narrator comments ironically that Ralph, Piggy and the twins Samneric are shaking convulsively as they remember 'the dance that none of them had attended.' (152,24)

2. What strategies does Jack employ to keep his followers under control? (153,33–155,28)

Jack exercises his absolute power in an arbitrary, destructive and threatening way. Thus Wilfred is beaten and tied up to satisfy the dictator's desire for torture and power. Furthermore, Jack plays on the superstitious fears of the others in order to keep them obediently in line. He stimulates and exploits their fears of the beast to establish a closed society based on fear and terror, because "the beast might try to come." (154,13) "Then if he comes we'll do our ... dance again." (155,25–26) Jack is now only referred to as 'The Chief'. (154,8/11/29/33) The Chief manipulates his gang in a subtle way, simultaneously justifying the need for ritual, obedience, authority and control in order to combat the beast.

In any dictatorship the political methods of keeping citizens under control are similar:

- playing on the fears of assumed enemies, scapegoats or hostile states,
- terror against political dissidents as a deterrent against political opposition,
- absolute control of social life,
- political propaganda and mass rituals,
- psychological conditioning and military rearmament for a war against 'the enemy.'

3. Comment on the significance of Roger's 'illumination'. (152,27–153,32)

Roger admires the 'proper Chief' (153,12) and the 'possibilities of irresponsible authority.' (153,30) This is like an 'illumination,' (153,29) releasing a sadistic impulse in Roger.

This contrasts with 'the taboo of the old life,' (60,12) when he was 'conditioned by a civilization' (60,14); however, this no longer prevents him from becoming a torturer and a killer in Jack's gang. When he considers the possibility of sending a huge rock 'thundering down,' (153,10) it becomes clear that later he will use the lever mechanism in order to kill Piggy.

4. Why does Jack steal Piggy's glasses? (155,29–162,9)

Piggy's glasses mean sight and stand for intellect, clear-sightedness and rational vision. The glasses are also an important means of lighting a signal fire for a possible rescue and for the provision of comfort, warmth and security.

When Jack manages to steal Piggy's glasses, he is joyous, 'exulting in his achievement.' (162,7) With Piggy's glasses, Jack completes his absolute and destructive power. 'He was a chief now in truth.' (162,7)

"The theft of Piggy's glasses might be interpreted as the defeat of the intellectual by the savage." (Kaiser 60)

Chapter 11: Castle Rock

Summary Headlines

1. Ralph, Piggy and Samneric realize that their position is hopeless and that without Piggy's glasses they cannot make a signal fire for rescue. So they decide to go to Jack's tribe at Castle Rock in order to negotiate some sort of agreement. (163,1–167,2)
2. At Castle Rock Ralph blows the conch for an assembly and accuses Jack of being a thief. A fierce fight between Jack and Ralph is interrupted by Piggy, who holds out the conch, accusing the angry and vicious crowd of irrational behaviour and imploring them to revert to civilized values. (167,3– 173,24)
3. Roger dislodges a huge rock which strikes Piggy and kills him instantly. The conch is smashed into fragments, Ralph escapes but is wounded by Jack's spear. The twins are captured. (173,25–175,18)

Significance

1. Ralph's and Piggy's final desperate appeal to reason, humanity and civilized life fails, because Jack still wields his authoritarian power unremittingly, and the hysterical and mindless crowd responds with fierce aggression.
2. In mutual consent with the mad crowd and its dictator, Roger, the unscrupulous executioner, kills Piggy.
3. Piggy's cruel death coincides with the breaking of the conch, the symbol of democratic and civilized order.

Guides for Analysis

1. How do Ralph, Piggy and the twins react after the raid?
2. Analyse the atmosphere that is created on the way to Castle Rock.
3. Comment on the relationship between Ralph and Jack.
4. Analyse Piggy's speech, the reaction of the crowd and Roger's behaviour.
5. Consider the significance of Piggy's death.

45

1. How do Ralph, Piggy and the twins react after the raid?
(163,1–167,2)

In this chapter the total defeat of rationality and civilization is demonstrated.

During the small assembly which follows, Ralph puts the blame for the boys' savagery entirely on Jack—"that's his fault." (164,10) Ralph claims that "after all we aren't savages really." (164,22) He denies any participation in Simon's murder, claiming also that he has not become a savage. And he naively proposes "to smarten up a bit and then go," (164,25) "looking like we used to, washed and hair brushed." (164,21–22) Ralph seeks to remind Jack and his savages of their earlier civilized, orderly and humane life. His repeated suggestion of washing away the dirt and of tidying up symbolically reflects his desire for a return to innocence.

Without his glasses Piggy is almost blind behind 'the luminous wall of his myopia.' (163,5) But he is now able to understand reality more clearly and to admit that Simon was murdered, obviously conceding his share of the guilt. Piggy assumes that Jack and his people will respect the authority of civilization represented by the conch which he will carry 'against all odds.' (165,28) He wants to appeal for morality and justice, "what's right's right." (165,9) But Piggy overestimates the authority of the 'fragile' (165,14) conch, which to Jack seems completely irrelevant, since civilized life no longer exists in his regime.

It should also be noted that Sam and Eric are tempted to imitate the painting and masking of the savages and that they even feel intrigued by 'the liberation into savagery that the conceiling paint brought.' (166,12–13) The irrational and savage behaviour of an anonymous crowd seems to attract them.

2. Analyse the atmosphere that is created on the way to Castle Rock.
(167,3–169,19)

On Ralph's and Piggy's way to the Castle Rock an atmosphere of danger and menace is created. The 'heat haze' (167,5) creates an oppressive atmosphere; the 'plate-like shadows' (167,12) seem to be sinister; 'the place where the tribe had danced' (167,18) reminds them of Simon's murder; 'a red, weedy square forty feet beneath' (168,8–9) is significant: Piggy will be smashed onto it later. Peering anxiously into the 'luminous veil that hung between him and the world,' (168,3–4) Piggy senses the danger they are facing.

When Roger takes a small stone and throws it between the twins, aiming to miss, the scene is quite similar to an earlier incident when Roger secretly throws stones at little Henry. (60,8–15)

Now an evil power begins 'to pulse in Roger's body,' (169,7) foreshadowing forthcoming cruel events.

3. Comment on the relationship between Ralph and Jack. (169,20–172,34)

When Jack appears, his individual identity is completely concealed. He is hardly recognizable. Ralph 'gazed at the green and black mask before him, trying to remember what Jack looked like.' (171,9–10)

Ralph's appeal to Jack's common sense, to his sense of justice and to his moral conscience fails.

On the contrary, Jack pretends to be offended — "Say that again!" (170,9) — reacting brutally, making a stab at Ralph with his spear, then later ordering "Grab them (i.e. the twins)!" (172,1), "Tie them up!" (172,10).

Jack is so proud of his absolute power over his mindless and obedient tribe that he can boast: "See? They do what I want." (172,21)

Ralph is outraged and completely disillusioned with Jack and calls him "a beast and a swine and a bloody, bloody thief!" (172,26)

He does not call him a murderer, nor does he mention Simon's death, because he might then be reminded of his own guilt. When Ralph and Jack fight, they are 'by common consent ... using the spears as sabres now, no longer daring the lethal points.' (170,20–22) This shows that Jack does not dare to hurt or kill Ralph. Jack's destructive urge is still restrained by a common consent not to kill Ralph. But these restraints will be abandoned after the murder of Piggy. Then the dictator sets out to hunt and kill his political opponent.

4. Analyse Piggy's speech, the reaction of the crowd and Roger's behaviour. (173,1–174,3)

The following passage is a highlight of narrative suspense. In order to reach a dramatic climax three views are paralleled and interwoven:
- Piggy's powerful speech and his final unsuccessful plea for common sense and reason,
- the fierce behaviour of the crowd and
- the view of Roger, the executioner.

Piggy accuses the savages of acting "like a crowd of kids" (173,16) and he contrasts reason, common sense and civilization with irrationality and savagery":

"Which is better—to be a pack of painted niggers like you are, or to be sensible like Ralph is? ...
Which is better—to have rules and agree, or to hunt and kill? ...
Which is better, law and rescue, or hunting and breaking things up?" (173,18–24)

During his speech Piggy holds out the conch almost desperately and imploringly against the crowd, the 'solid mass of menace.' (173,26–27)

The conch, however, is of extremely 'fragile, shining beauty' (173,30–31), and serves as a contrast to the ugliness of this grim society and also foreshadows its destruction.

The crowd responds to Piggy's speech with cheering, curious silence and mockery, then booing, clamour and hysterical yelling. Finally the 'intention of a charge was forming among them.' (173,27–28) The crowd is like the 'incantation of hatred' (173,31–32) now.

From Roger's distant vantage point uphill, Ralph is 'a shock of hair' (173,14) and Piggy, his victim, 'a bag of fat.' (173,14–15) During Piggy's speech, Roger—with his hand on the lever mechanism—is throwing stones. But when the crowd is ready to charge, Roger becomes the executioner. With 'a sense of delirious abandonment' (173,32) Roger leans all his weight on the lever that dislodges a huge rock, which kills Piggy and destroys the conch.

Roger, who at the beginning of the novel was described as the 'furtive boy whom no one knew,' (20,15) has become a killer—'the hangman's horror clung round him.' (175,5)

5. Consider the significance of Piggy's death. (174,4–175,18)

Piggy's murder is a brutal and cruel act of violence. Whereas Simon's death is described in an almost metaphysical way, Piggy's death is described in a matter-of-fact way like the slaughtering of a pig: 'The rock struck Piggy a glancing blow from chin to knee; ... with no time for even a grunt ... His head opened and stuff came out and turned red. Piggy's arms and legs twitched a bit, like a pig's after it has been killed.' (174,4–11)

Piggy's death is seen from the rather detached perspective of someone—possibly Roger or Jack—who has already been accustomed to slaughtering and killing. The unemotional and neutral language makes Piggy's violent death even more terrible and horrifying.

Thus, terror, violence and even murder have ultimately become a daily routine in Jack's totalitarian society.

Piggy's murder coincides with the breaking of the conch, the symbol of democratic and civilized order. The destruction of Piggy and the conch is the defeat of that order and the starting point of unrestrained violence and terror.

From that moment on Jack is ready to kill Ralph. The screaming mob with 'the anonymous devils' faces' (174,27–28) are ready to assist him.

Chapter 12: Cry of the Hunters

Summary Headlines

1. Ralph is wounded by Jack's spear and hunted down by the savages. (176,1–177,27)
2. Ralph encounters the Lord of the Flies and tries to destroy 'him'. (177,28–178,19)
3. The twins, Samneric, warn Ralph of Jack's cruel policy and that Ralph's head might soon replace the pig's. (178,19–183,23)
4. Ralph is running for his life, chased like an animal. The island is set on fire and huge rocks are sent down to kill Ralph. Finally, in a situation where no escape is possible and in complete despair and helplessness, Ralph tries to cry for mercy. (183,25–191,24)
5. The huge fire has destroyed nearly the whole island but has also alarmed a British warship, which finally rescues Ralph and the other boys. (191,25–193,33)

Significance

1. In the final chapter of the novel a number of cross-references to earlier similar incidents are made. In the context of the climax of the story, these earlier incidents foreshadow psychological threat, physical menace, violence, terror, destruction and murder.
2. The metaphorical significance of the scar in the jungle (chapter 1) and the scar on Ralph's ribs (chapter 12) reveals that human beings are responsible for the suffering of nature and the suffering of other human beings.
3. The mass which is unrestrained by human values and encouraged by a totalitarian regime is going to kill its opponents.
4. By the end, Ralph has gained a fundamental knowledge of the conflict of good and evil and has come to know people's potential for brutality, violence and savagery.
5. The rescue is ambiguous and does not indicate a purely happy ending, because the adult world is at war and the boys will be taken back to that world.

Guides for Analysis

1. Explain the metaphorical significance of 'the scar.'
2. Analyse Ralph's psychological situation.
3. How does Ralph's encounter with the Lord of the Flies differ from Simon's?
4. Analyse the significance of cross-references to earlier incidents.
5. Analyse the ending of the novel.

1. Explain the metaphorical significance of 'the scar'.
(176,1–177,5)

Ralph escapes and hides from the savages. He feels like a hunted and terrified animal. He is wounded and suffers from a bloody scar where Jack has hit him with his spear. Ralph's bloody scar resembles the 'long scar smashed into the jungle' (5,4–5) by the crashing aeroplane mentioned at the beginning of the novel.

The metaphorical link between the scar in the jungle and the scar on Ralph's ribs reveals a striking parallel:

On the one hand, nature has been wounded by the intrusion of man, on the other hand, the suffering individual has been deliberately wounded by his fellow people.

In both cases the scars are caused by human beings, the message being that people are responsible for the destruction of nature as well as for the suffering of other people.

2. Analyse Ralph's psychological situation. (177,6–27)

Ralph ignores the truth and tries to deceive himself about Jack's cruel intentions. He does not want to acknowledge that he will be the next victim of Jack's regime. He deceives himself into thinking that Jack and his tribe are not "as bad as that" (177,14) and that Piggy's death was only "an accident." (177,14) Here, his attitude is quite similar to Piggy's earlier self-deceiving attitude towards Simon's murder. And Ralph therefore decides to 'ignore this leaden feeling about the heart and rely on their common sense, their daylight sanity.' (177,21–22)

Ralph is aware of an 'indefinable connection between himself and Jack' (177,10–11) that has already been indicated in an earlier incident, when Ralph and Jack 'looked at each other, baffled, in love and hate.' (53,12)

This shows that the two antagonists are still closely connected to each other: Ralph has a streak of potential violence that was released when he took part in Simon's murder. Jack, on the other hand, wants to get rid of his opponent, who keeps reminding him of civilized and humane values.

"Ralph has something of Jack in him, and Jack will never be really free from Ralph and the standards that he represents until Ralph is dead." (Kaiser 64)

3. How does Ralph's encounter with the Lord of the Flies differ from Simon's? (177,28–178,18)

When Ralph encounters the Lord of the Flies, the scene parallels and contrasts Simon's encounter with it. The skull jeers at him 'cynically' (177,35) and—like Simon—Ralph is aware of a 'cynicism' (133,7) of life. The narrator's comment on Ralph's perception is significant: 'The skull regarded Ralph like one who knows all the answers and won't tell.' (178,6–7) This suggests that Ralph should know the real reason for the boys' savage behaviour, which is 'the beast' in human nature, in himself. Whereas Simon understood the message of the Lord of the Flies, Ralph rejects this message. With fear and rage, Ralph lashes out at the pig's head in fury and tries to destroy its cynical grin. But ironically he only succeeds in magnifying the grin, 'now six feet across.' (178,11)

4. Analyse the significance of cross-references to earlier incidents. (178,19–191,24)

Ralph has become the victim of evil forces which close in on him. The following cross-references to earlier incidents are significant and reinforce the psychological threat and physical menace to the people concerned.

Ralph hides in exactly the same space that was smashed by the great rock which killed Piggy. 'When Ralph had wriggled into this he felt secure, and clever.' (184,7–8) But when he is discovered, the savages respond with a 'silvery laughter' (184,28) that resembles the menace of the 'shivering, silvery, unreal laughter' (171,20/172,5) that rang out earlier.

The reaction of the savages shows their cruelty and complete loss of responsibility.

Huge rocks are sent crashing down in order to kill Ralph. The rocks smash scars through the thicket and one huge rock, 'big as a car, a tank' (185,17) nearly kills Ralph, who is 'shot into the air, thrown down, dashed against branches.' (185,31–32) Here, the parallel to the falling-rock incident in chapter one (26,8–31) and to the murder of Piggy is obvious. The brutal killing strategy has definitely been elaborated. Piggy was killed 'in delirious abandonment' (173,32) by an individual sadist, Ralph is tracked down by a vicious crowd and its dictator with calculated intent.

"A rule of terror imposes its own arbitrary terms: it is about torture and power … least of all about justice and reason." (Wilson 43)

Under attack in his hide-out, Ralph throws his spear in panic and self-defence, hurting one of the boys. Ralph feels and acts like a hunted animal. The description particularly resembles the scene when Ralph hits and wounds a boar (109,27–110,10). Now he is the boar: he 'snarled' (187,3) 'like a boar' (187,27) and desperately foresees that 'the hunt would become a running down.' (187,25–26) He even 'wondered if a pig would agree.' (188,35)

When the savages deliberately set the forest on fire, the smoke and the 'drum-roll' (189,16/45,21) of the rapidly spreading fire does not signify rescue but destruction. The bursting trees resemble the first fire on the island that got out of control and in which the young boy with the birthmark died. When Ralph is in despair and even tries to think reasonably, 'what would they eat tomorrow,' (189,36) this recalls Piggy's reproach during the second assembly: "Won't we look funny if the whole island burns up? Cooked fruit, that's what we'll have to eat, and roast pork." (44,13–15) The whole tragic impact of Piggy's slightly amusing reproach has become reality in the final part of the novel.

When Ralph realizes that the stick he has taken from the Lord of the Flies is 'sharpened at both ends' (190,2–3), he now understands Samneric's earlier warning—"Roger sharpened a stick at both ends" (182,23); this means that Ralph's head might replace the pig's soon. Simon's earlier prophetic words—'You'll get back' (190,35/180,4/11/20) now seem to be totally wrong. Ralph runs for his life like a desperate pig, 'screaming, snarling, bloody' (191,2) with the savages chasing him, like a 'jagged fringe of menace.' (191,18)

"All the concentric circles of the novel now close in on Ralph—identified with the pig and the place—in a climactic high tide of evil that threatens to engulf him and the island alike. He has become the prey of the evil force which he had so far observed from the outside." (Delbaere-Garant 85)

Ralph is helpless and in despair, 'crouching with arm up to ward off, trying to cry for mercy.' (191,23–24) And this, in fact, could have been one possible ending of the novel.

5. Analyse the ending of the novel. (191,25–193,33)

The surprise ending to Lord of the Flies can be analysed as the end of a nightmare, with the naval officer as 'deus ex machina', but equally as a return to civilization and to critical self-awareness:

"what happens is like turning on the lights in the theatre before the curtains close, and then letting the cast suddenly step outside the action that had mesmerized us. We are forced to distance the completed experience, and measure how far we have travelled." (Kinkead-Weeks 62)

The boys are rescued, because—ironically—the huge fire that has nearly destroyed the whole island has alarmed a British warship.

The naval officer views the situation as "fun and games" (192,13): Ralph is a 'little scarecrow' (192,21) in need of 'a nose-wipe and a good deal of ointment.' (192,21–22) Jack is a 'little boy' with the remnant of a black cap and 'the remains of a pair of spectacles at his waist.' (193,5–6) The rest of the boys are 'tiny tots.' (192,30)

In his uncomprehending and even condescending pose, the naval officer compares the "pack of British boys" (193,12) to Ballantyne's romantic heroes: "Jolly good show. Like the Coral Island." (193,19/ compare 203–204)

But the revolver, the cutter with the sub-machine gun and the trim cruiser represent the military weapons of an adult world at war, and not at all peaceful and civilized.

"In terms of meaning, symbol and morality, the implications of Golding's perspective are clear: the central darkness and evil the boys revealed reflects a larger human darkness and evil, … a world at war violating the false confidence of progressive and civilized values." (Gindin 29)

In his moment of recognition, Ralph weeps for 'the end of innocence, the darkness of man's heart, and the fall through the air of the true, wise friend called Piggy.' (193,28–30) Ralph has matured and acquired an essential knowledge of mankind. He understands the conflict of good and evil that exists in man. He has come to know people's potential for brutality and violence towards their fellow human beings. He has become aware of the potential evil forces lying behind people's innocent appearance and that—metaphorically—'the beast' does not exist outside people but within them.

William Golding:

"By the end, he has come to understand the fallen nature of man, and that what stands between him and happiness comes from inside him." (200,18–20)

An interview with Sir William Golding

BAKER: Speaking of formative influences, there was a period after you left Oxford in 1934, a rather obscure or lost period, when you got into theater, into acting.

GOLDING: Well, it was a sort of fringe theatre, I wouldn't dignify it by the name of acting. It was the Hampstead Everyman Theatre, Citizen House at Bath, and trifling things of that sort. It would be an impertinence on my part to say that I was part of the professional stage scene because I wasn't. I was a hanger-on round the fringes and finally collapsed to the side, into teaching.

BAKER: But that does denote an interest in and an enthusiasm for drama and the theater itself.

GOLDING: I was more or less brought up on Shakespeare and that has an influence. Only recently I decided that I'd spent my life quoting Shakespeare to people, and I'm not going to do it anymore because everything you want to say you can say by using Shakespeare's words. What a bore I must have been over a period of about sixty years, solemnly quoting Shakespeare to people. They must have said, Oh, God, not again; can't he find his own words? So I've given it up, but there's no doubt that I know my Shakespeare pretty well by heart, and if you would like to consider that as denoting an interest in drama, I suppose it does.

BAKER: It seems to me there has been a strong influence of theatre and of drama in your own work. This is visible in *Pincher Martin*. It's visible again in, of course, your own play *The Brass Butterfly*. It's quite visible too in *Rites of Passage*.

GOLDING: *Rites of Passage* is, I suppose, pretty theatrical in a way, but then it had to be if you consider the problem, because the book is founded on an actual historical incident. (...)

BAKER: But the idea of theatre as a metaphor is very much a part of *Pincher Martin* as well. We have the man on the rock, a sort of poor actor in his own theatre of the mind.

GOLDING: Being his own Lear on the blasted heath and all that. Yes, I think that is so. But then what else is the theatre? It's a place for people to exhibit themselves. That's what an actor is, isn't he? Since people stopped wearing masks on their faces and went out and used their own, well, then they are actors and anybody who is putting on a show for the people is an actor. I remember a brilliant demonstration of the whole situation in Peter Brook's *Marat-Sade* which takes place in the lunatic asylum, and the people, the mad people are acting mad; and at the end when there is absolute hell let loose they all suddenly turn and rush down towards the audience and start applauding the audience like mad, or perhaps I should say applauding them loudly, because the real actors have been the audience sitting in their neat little rows, you know, and not coughing and doing exactly as they are told, having personas, these civilized frumps that are arranged there; whereas the real genuine people are these mad people who've let everything go and so they're applauding us, the audience, for our splendid acting. It was brilliant, I thought. Most effective.

BAKER: While the impact of World War II on your own life and on your work I suppose is well enough known …

GOLDING: I think so.

BAKER: Since we have spoken of those things before, I wanted to ask you whether *Free Fall* is something of a chronicle of the war years reflecting the spiritual crises of the time and whether Sammy, like all of us were in those years, is in a state of free fall, that is, without belief, without faith, without any system of belief. Is he a representative figure in other words?

GOLDING: (…) I do remember that my thesis, I think, was the fact that without a system of values, without an adherence to some, one might almost call it, codified morality, right and wrong, you are like a creature in space, tumbling, eternally tumbling, no up, no down, just in "free fall" in the scientific sense. (…) I've found the metaphor adequate for my purpose, the fact that man is, I believe, by nature a moral creature, and when he's in free fall he, so to speak, stumbles over his morals without knowing they are there. He exploits people and then finds that with this comes guilt and that you can't be free of right and wrong because you know by some kind of instinct when you've exploited somebody, when you've hurt somebody, when you've cheated somebody. You know when you lie and all the rest of it. It's no good saying none of these things matter. They do. They matter intensely to man because he is not just man, he is a social being.

BAKER: But you came out of the war and wrote *Lord of the Flies* and referred to man as a morally diseased creature, "a morally diseased creation."

GOLDING: Yes, I used that phrase, maybe I wouldn't now, maybe it's inexact, I wonder what I would say about him now. I remember being in a television program called "Brains Trust" about twenty years ago, more than that now, and I remember alluding in passing to the idea of original sin and I suppose allowing it to be inferred that I believed in original sin and somebody else there, a scientist, really got rather angry. I think it was Julian Huxley, actually, and he said all this talk about original sin is absolute nonsense, that man is a creature who suffers from an innate inability to live a proper and satisfactory life in a social circumstance. And I said, well, that's an elaborate definition of original sin. Our nature is to want to grab something that belongs to somebody else, and we have either to be taught or teach ourselves that you've got to share, you can't grab the lot. And for God's sake, history is really no more than a chronicle of original sin, I would have thought. (…)

BAKER: You must feel then that *Lord of the Flies* really determines your public image.

GOLDING: Yes.

BAKER: I mean in the sense that it overshadows the remainder of your work. The book has become a sort of tyrant.

GOLDING: I don't spend my time thinking about it. People, I suppose, tend to think of me as the person who wrote *Lord of the Flies*, but I don't think of myself as the person who wrote *Lord of the Flies*. I'm the person who has to live with me.

BAKER: When *Lord of the Flies* appeared the critics spoke of it as a fable and I remember, at the time, you said you would prefer to think of it as "mythic". Both of those words suggest something universal or general in reach, and of course that's accurate and true, but it was conceived in part as a book about Britain and the British, was it not?

GOLDING: Yes.

BAKER: And this has not been generally recognized or stressed in the critical commentary; it's partly about the class structure.

GOLDING: Not necessarily the British class structure. I mean it can be about the class structure, say in Russia or even in America, come to that, or anywhere. Every country has a class structure of some sort or another, and the same forces operate in it to one end or another. I knew about British boys, I was one myself; I know about British society, after all I've lived all my life in it. So it was natural I should take that rather than say, Sweden or South Africa or Australia or America or France. My thesis, I believe, would be this, that you could have taken any bunch of boys from any country and stuck them on an island and you would have ended up with mayhem.

BAKER: But again, that persistent theme in your work—the fall from innocence or the loss of innocence.

GOLDING: Well, it's quite a big theme, isn't it? It's rather like saying here's a novelist who writes about people. (…)

BAKER: But one of the traditional justifications for art is that it instructs us. The artist is a kind of disguised schoolmaster. He has something to tell us, something he *wants* to tell us.

GOLDING: I know, that's a traditional argument. It might be true, but on the other hand, it's a bit distressing to think of oneself as a sort of *domine* wielding a sort of cane in one hand and holding out a bribe in the other to pupils. I suppose one does say, not that way, but this. And of course the excuse for the horrible things that go on on the stage is purging through pity and terror, but I must confess that I've never understood what Aristotle was getting at with that. (…)

BAKER: May we now change subject and make some effort to place your work in tradition, in literary tradition? Could you speak to that, to that question, yourself?

GOLDING: I suppose all I can really say is that I don't think my novels come out of novels. If they owe anything to previous work, and obviously they must, it's the theatre much more than novel writing. It's great drama in particular. I think of the shape of a novel, when I do think of a novel as having a shape, as having a shape precisely like Greek drama. You have this rise of tension and then the sudden fall and all the rest of it. You may even find the technical Greek terms tucked away in the book, if you like, and check them off one by one. So the Greek tragedy as a form, a classical form, is very much there. The idea of the character who suffers a disastrous fall through a flaw in his character, that you find there, I think. So it does really stem as much from Greek tragedy as much as anything else.

William Golding was interviewed by James R. Baker. The interview was recorded at Golding's home near Salisbury, England, on June 5, 1981 and published in *Twentieth Century Literature*, Summer 1982, pp. 130–170.

Insights of a Man Apart

*James Wood meets the Nobel laureate William Golding
on his 80th birthday*

We speed through Wiltshire and Somerset, through the sloping, downy, polite countryside in which William Golding grew up and about which he has written, and down into Cornwall, the watery foot of England, where he now lives in expensive seclusion. He came here after winning the Nobel prize in 1983, to avoid the celebrity-tumult—the journalists, the academics, the literary lunchers. Here the countryside is rougher, edged and harried by the sea which is always close. Indeed, Golding's large and seigneurial house—with its creamy brick and gravel approach— is not far from the sea.

Golding comes out to meet me. He looks hieratic, pharisaical, a Noah, a Moses. His white hair is sparse and flossy; but his beard prospers wirily all over the chin and neck. So much hanging down from this face, so many roots and fronds—it makes Golding's face curiously alive, yet also dead, as if frozen and framed in whiteness. His Mandarin eyes have no lashes, and slope downwards. He is somewhat godly in manner. It is clear from the beginning that he is only moderately interested in politesse. "I don't give a damn what yo do," he replies to my question about a tape recorder. I'm put on edge of course; I feel the soles of my feet tighten as I follow him indoors.

Golding's writing is also somewhat godly. His prose is stony, and difficult, as if written on high-minded tablets. He has no voice, no personal tone. Though majestic and in some ways visionary, his novels are astoundingly unworldly. His fiction is a stranger to the fleshly, the robust, the contemporary. "I wouldn't know how to begin to write about contemporary society," he confesses to me at one point. Instead, he goes back into history and into closed societies—an island *(Lord of the Flies)*, a cathedral *(The Spire)*, a ship *(Rites of Passage)*. Moreover, his vision is curiously static. He believes, as he puts it in his essay "Fable", that man produces evil as the bee produces honey. We are original sinners. He is a religious novelist, yet there is little sense in his work of dialectic, or even argument. His vision appears to be made up of blocks and formations of belief. Correspondingly, he has a weakness for the literary equivalent of such blocks—symbols. One thinks of the conch (which stands for parliamentary democracy) in *Lord of the Flies;* or the spire in his novel of that name (which stands for hubris, knowledge, a man's phallus); or the ship in *Rites of Passage* (which stands for nothing less than the ship of life). He has said "The important thing is not that man exists, but that God exists," which may be saintly in a believer, but is surely heretical in a novelist. (...)

Golding's fiction abounds in such moments of vision; indeed, his fiction is essentially about vision, about finally seeing goodness, evil, and the loss of innocence. Many of his characters—Ralph in *Lord of the Flies,* Jocelin, *Oliver in the Pyramid*—have a sudden visionary access at the end of his books. "Jocelin," says Golding, "realises at the end that there is no innocent work. His spire has been erected for shabby reasons. He is a proud man. I suppose that sense of innocence polluted runs through my fiction." It may be that Golding's acute sense of this pollution has in part to do with his background. He grew up in Marlborough, in Wiltshire, a kind of rural quarantine, an innocent English idyll (it becomes the village of Stilbourne in *The Pyramid*). Golding's parents lived in an old house on the Green, next to the churchyard, and he has written powerfully about his childish discovery that bodies, stacked on the other side of his garden wall, were lying pointed into the family garden. (...)

One of Golding's most recent novels, *The Paper Men,* was all about people like me. The book grew out of Golding's irritation with researchers, academics, and literary journalists. World famous, he felt tormented and invaded by such types. (...)

The cause of all this unpleasantness is one book, *Lord of the Flies.* Since the late fifties, the book has gone before him, waving a red flag, wherever he has gone. On campuses, in lecture halls, in interviews, Golding has elucidated its messages, unravelled its complexities. He has written many novels since *Lord of the Flies,* but for millions of readers he exists in a kind of haze or fog of celebrity: no new information can be allowed to disturb this cloudy aura—William Golding is the author of one book. He is tired of talking about it—he wrote the essay "Fable" as a way of "answering some of the standard questions which students were asking me"—and yet, strangely enough, it is only when he begins to talk to me about it that he becomes at all mobile or enthusiastic. "It's gone on selling since the day it was published. God knows how many copies it's sold—10 million, 15 million? I suppose I should be eternally grateful to those students who turned it into a campus novel in the late fifties. Because they kept on buying it. And those students, of course, are now the professors who are writing books about it."

The story of the genesis of *Lord of the Flies* is now well known: how it was rejected by numerous publishers and plucked from the reject pile at Faber by Charles Monteith. I asked Golding if he had any sense then, that he had written a classic novel. "Yes I did, I think. I'd already written three novels which no one had published, and which I knew weren't any good. I thought, this one must succeed. And so I constructed it very carefully. It sounds terribly naive, but one of my discoveries had been that in a novel something has to happen. So I went through the final manuscript with a pen, ticking each point at which something happened. This accounts for its very plotted and urgent feel ..." But the novel was rejected again and again. "I sat down and re-read it, and said to my wife 'This is bloody good.' I also said to myself privately, 'One day this book will win me the Nobel prize'. And was instantly appalled by my pride. But you see, I knew it was good."

Talking about his early struggles, Golding comes to life. His eyes soften, the atmosphere warms. We're no longer sitting in our stiff little chamber, but in a writer's drawingroom, with a mild and unemphatic afternoon light streaming through the window and making columns and spokes of dust. Golding seems to shed some of his priestliness and to take on a humble glow. At last, a writer sits before me—the sum of his struggles, the sum of his difficult knowledge and curious isolation—not an institution, not a busy Nobel laureate. And this new humility seems right, for humility runs through Golding's work as a virtue, a prize. Humility is what the schoolboy dictators of the island in *Lord of the Flies* learn at the end of the book; humility comes to Pincher Martin, hanging on his purgatorial rock; humility amongst broken images is the cross which Jocelin must carry at the end of *The Spire*. Some of this humility also belongs to Golding. I ask him about his work as a whole, and he says this, shifting slightly in his chair, and gazing gently into his lap: "Looking at my work, I realise what a slight and inadequate body it is. I totted my books up the other day—16 volumes after 80 years. That's my lot, essentially. It's not much is it? I envy those who have produced 30 or 40 books. I would call this body of work trivial. So naturally, I'm still looking for the ultimate novel. I have still to write my best book." (...)

James Wood, in: *Guardian Weekly*, September 29, 1991.

Selected Bibliography

Howard S. Babb, *The Novels of William Golding*. (Ohio State University Press) Columbus 1970.

Coles Editorial Board, *Golding. Lord of the Flies. Notes*. Toronto 1989.

Jeanne Delbaere-Garant, "Rhythm and Expansion in Lord of the Flies" in: *William Golding, Some Critical Considerations*. Ed. by Jack I. Biles/Robert O. Evans, Lexington, Kentucky 1978, pp. 72–86.

Terence Dewsnap, *William Golding's Lord of the Flies and The Inheritors, Pincher Martin, Free Fall. A Guide to Understanding the Classics*. (Monarch Notes) New York 1964.

James Gindin, *William Golding*. Macmillian Modern Novelists, London 1988.

William Golding, "Fable" in: *The Hot Gates* by William Golding, London 1965, pp. 85–90.

William Golding, "Nobel Lecture" in: *A Moving Target* by William Golding, London 1984, pp. 211–213.

Arnold Johnston, *Of Earth and Darkness. The Novels of William Golding*. (University of Missouri Press), Columbia and London 1980.

Gerd Kaiser, *Stundenblätter—Golding "Lord of the Flies"*. (Ernst Klett Verlag), Stuttgart 1985.

Mark Kinkead-Weekes/Ian Gregor, *William Golding. A Critical Study*. London 1984.

W. Meitcke, *Lektürehilfen—William Golding "Lord of the Flies"*. (Ernst Klett Verlag/Barron's Book Notes), Stuttgart 1987.

William Nelson, *William Golding's Lord of the Flies—A Source Book*. (The Odyssey Press), Indianapolis/New York 1963.

Alastair Niven, *William Golding, Lord of the Flies*. (York Notes/Longman York Press) Harlow, Essex 1980.

Dieter Smolka, "William Golding: Lord of the Flies. A Classical Novel Revisited" in: *Fremdsprachenunterricht* Nr. 5/96, Sept./Okt. 1996, pp. 337–341.

Virginia Tiger, *William Golding. The Dark Fields of Discovery*. London 1974.

Rudolf Ulrich, "Der Roman im Leistungskurs Englisch. Möglichkeiten zu seiner Behandlung im Unterricht aufgezeigt an vier Beispielstunden zu Goldings Lord of the Flies." in: Hans-Jürgen Diller u. a. Hrsg., *Anglistik und Englischunterricht*. Bd. 12, Bochum/Trier 1980, S. 77–102.

Hermann J. Weiand, "William Golding, Lord of the Flies" in: *Insight V, Analyses of Twentieth-Century British and American Fiction*. Edited by Hermann J. Weiand, Frankfurt/M. 1981, pp. 88–105.

John S. Whitley, *Golding: Lord of the Flies*. (Edward Arnold Publisher), London 1983.

Raymond Wilson, *Lord of the Flies by William Golding*. (Macmillan Master Guides), London 1986.

9 8765 43